I Like Biographies!

Read About
Crazy Horse

Stephen Feinstein

Enslow Elementary
an imprint of
Enslow Publishers, Inc.

40 Industrial Road   PO Box 38
Box 398   Aldershot
Berkeley Heights, NJ 07922 Hants GU12 6BP
USA   UK

http://www.enslow.com

Words to Know

Oglala Sioux (Oh-GLA-la Soo)—An Indian tribe that lived on the Great Plains of North America.

reservation—Land set aside by the government for a special purpose.

treaty—A written and signed agreement.

vision—Something seen in a dream.

vision quest—A search for a vision.

warrior—A person who fights in battles.

Enslow Elementary, an imprint of Enslow Publishers, Inc.

Enslow Elementary® is a registered trademark of Enslow Publishers, Inc.

Copyright © 2005 by Enslow Publishers, Inc.

Library of Congress Cataloging-in-Publication Data

Feinstein, Stephen.

   Read about Crazy Horse / Stephen Feinstein.
      p. cm. — (I like biographies!)
   Includes bibliographical references and index.
   ISBN 0-7660-2590-X
   1. Crazy Horse, ca. 1842–1877—Juvenile literature.
2. Oglala Indians—Kings and rulers—Biography—Juvenile literature. 3. Little Bighorn, Battle of the, Mont., 1876—Juvenile literature. I. Title. II. Series.
   E99.O3C722133 2005
   978.004'975244'0092—dc22
      [B]
                           2004010622

Printed in the United States of America

10 9 8 7 6 5 4 3 2 1

To Our Readers: We have done our best to make sure all Internet Addresses in this book were active and appropriate when we went to press. However, the author and the publisher have no control over and assume no liability for the material available on those Internet sites or on links to other Web sites. Any comments or suggestions can be sent by e-mail to comments@enslow.com or to the address on the back cover.

Illustration Credits: Artville, LLC, p. 19; Clipart.com, p. 22; Corel Corp., pp. 3, 5, 13; *Crazy Horse* 1/34th scale model, Korczak, sculptor, © Crazy Horse Memorial Foundation, p. 21; Paul Daly, p. 1; Library of Congress, pp. 11, 15, 17; National Archives and Records Administration, p. 9; Charles M. Russell, "Buffalo Hunt #26," 1899, oil on canvas, 1961.206, © Amon Carter Museum, Fort Worth, Tex., p. 7.

Cover Illustration: Painting by Carl Feryok.

Contents

Chapter 1

The Boy With Curly Hair

Crazy Horse was born about 1841 in the Black Hills of South Dakota. His parents were from the Oglala Sioux tribe. They named their child Curly because of his curly hair.

When Curly was a boy, he did not speak much. But when he did, others listened. Curly's friends followed wherever he led.

Like these Indians, Curly and his friends rode their ponies far out across the plains. They practiced using their bows and arrows.

When Curly was twelve, he took part in his first buffalo hunt. Curly rode his horse into the middle of the herd. He took aim and shot an arrow into a buffalo. The huge animal fell to the ground. Curly was happy that his tribe would have plenty to eat.

Curly learned to become a good hunter. He and his friends were eager to become warriors, too.

While Curly was growing up and learning the ways of his tribe, new people were moving into the Indian lands. White settlers traveled west in long wagon trains.

To protect the settlers, the Army built a fort. The Indians were not happy because their land was being taken away.

White people came from far away and settled on Indian lands. This family traveled to Nebraska in their covered wagon.

One day Curly visited the camp of a friendly tribe. The people there were sad. They said a white man's cow had come into the camp. An Indian killed the cow. Chief Conquering Bear said he would give the white man a horse in return. But he refused the offer.

Soldiers from the fort then attacked the camp. They killed many Indians, including the chief.

The Oglala Sioux Indians lived in tepees like this one. So did the Brulé Sioux, the friendly tribe that Curly visited.

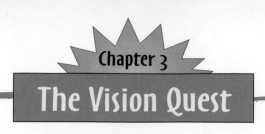
Curly was worried about what might happen to his people. How could he help protect them? He thought a vision would give him the answer.

Curly went to a place high above the river to be alone. He sat there for three days and nights. He had nothing to eat or drink. No vision came.

In this painting, the Indians are watching a wagon train. Curly was worried about having white people come to his land.

13

Suddenly, Curly saw a man riding a horse across the sky. In his vision, bullets filled the air, but the man kept on riding.

Curly's father told him that the man on the horse was Curly. He would become the leader of his people. He would fight for them. Later, Curly's father gave him a new name—Crazy Horse.

Curly went to a cliff like this one high above the river. This picture of Echo Canyon in South Dakota was taken in 1891, long after Crazy Horse lived.

Chapter 4

Crazy Horse Defends His People

Crazy Horse became a leader of the Oglala Sioux. He did all he could to save his people and their way of life. The Indians were being forced to give up their old ways.

The United States government broke every treaty it made with the Indians. Tribes gave up their lands and moved to reservations. But they did not receive the food and supplies they had been promised.

These chiefs are from different Indian tribes. The Indians made agreements with the American government. But the government broke the treaties.

17

In 1875, the government told Crazy Horse and his people to move onto a reservation. He said no. The following year, Crazy Horse won big battles against the army. At the Battle of the Little Bighorn, George A. Custer and all of his soldiers were killed.

This map shows the area where Crazy Horse lived. Fort Laramie is where the Brulé Sioux were killed, and the Little Bighorn is where the Indians defeated Custer's army.

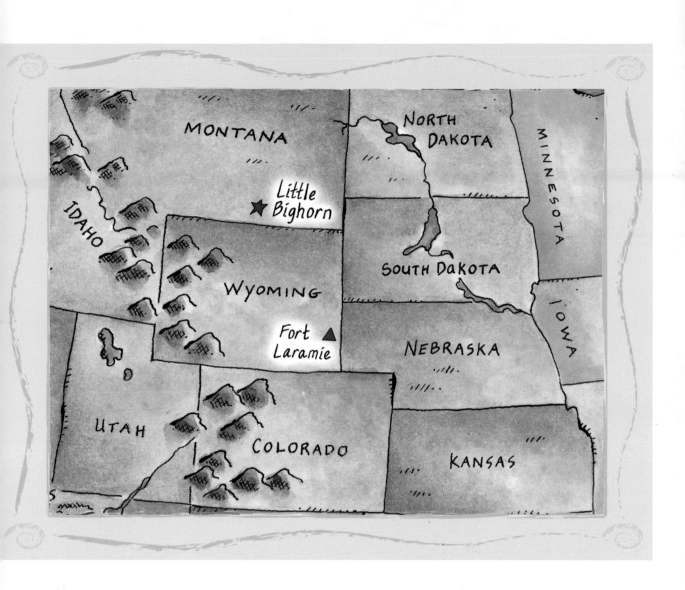

On September 5, 1877, Crazy Horse rode into Fort Robinson, Nebraska. He had come to make peace. But soldiers tried to put him into a jail cell. One of them stabbed Crazy Horse in the back. The brave Indian chief died the next day.

Today a huge figure of Crazy Horse is being carved out of a mountain in the Black Hills in South Dakota.

This picture shows the carving of Crazy Horse. The model in front shows what the carving will look like when it is finished.

© Crazy Horse Memorial Foundation

21

Timeline

About 1841—Curly is born in the Black Hills of what is now South Dakota.

1854—Curly goes on his vision quest.

1865—Crazy Horse becomes a leader of the Oglala Sioux.

1876—Crazy Horse's warriors and other Indians defeat George A. Custer and his army at the Battle of the Little Bighorn.

1877—Crazy Horse is killed.

Learn More

Books

Birchfield, D. L. *Crazy Horse*. Austin, Tex.: Raintree Steck-Vaughn, 2003.

Bruchac, Joseph. *Crazy Horse's Vision*. New York: Lee & Low Books, 2000.

Koestler-Grack, Rachel A. *The Sioux: Nomadic Buffalo Hunters*. Mankato, Minn.: Blue Earth Books, 2003.

Kotzwinkle, William. *The Return of Crazy Horse*. Berkeley, Calif.: North Atlantic, 2001.

Internet Addresses

Crazy Horse Memorial Foundation
<http://www.crazyhorse.org>

"Crazy Horse: Story of a Brave Sioux Leader"
<http://www.brownvboard.org/brwnqurt/02-4/02-4c.htm>

Index